US SMALL ARMS IN WORLD WAR II

A PHOTOGRAPHIC HISTORY OF THE WEAPONS IN ACTION

US SMALL ARMS IN WORLD WAR II

A PHOTOGRAPHIC HISTORY OF THE WEAPONS IN ACTION

TOM LAEMLEIN

FOREWORD BY CAPTAIN DALE DYE, USMC (ret.)

LAYOUT AND DESIGN BY MIKE GERENSER

First published in Great Britain in 2011 by Osprey Publishing,
Midland House, West Way, Botley, Oxford, OX2 0PH, UK
44-02 23rd Street, Suite 219, Long Island City, NY 11101, USA

E-mail: info@ospreypublishing.com

A CIP catalog record for this book is available from the British Library

Print ISBN: 978 1 84908 494 9

Page layout by Mike Gerenser
Typeset in Bembo

Originated by PPS Grasmere Ltd, Leeds, UK
Printed in China through Worldprint

11 12 13 14 10 9 8 7 6 5 4 3 2 1

Osprey Publishing is supporting the Woodland Trust, the UK's leading woodland conservation charity, by funding the dedication of trees.

www.ospreypublishing.com

Contents

Foreword

BY CAPTAIN DALE DYE, USMC (ret.)

Surviving veterans of infantry combat in the European Theater of Operations or in the Pacific will likely arch a shaggy eyebrow or two over the title of Tom Laemlein's insightful new pictorial essay on US small arms in World War II. To hear them tell it – and many more of them are willing to do so at this point sixty-plus years after the end of that war – there was nothing small about the arms they used to defeat the German and Japanese enemy at close quarters from 1941 to 1945. To them, the pistols, rifles, carbines, shotguns, submachine and machine guns were the largest things in their lives as they struggled to survive and succeed on battlefields from North Africa to Europe and across the broad expanses of the Pacific.

Down in the rifle platoons of the letter companies of the average World War II infantry battalion – Army or Marine Corps – there was an admixture of types that brought a variety of back-stories and experiences to their service up on the pointy-end of the bayonet. There were city kids from rough-and-tumble urban neighborhoods who knew the grafters and gangsters that never went anywhere without a pistol tucked somewhere handy. There were country boys who grew up hunting birds with scatterguns and squirrels with small-caliber rifles. And there were those from somewhere in between that plinked at the neighbor's cat with BB guns and cheered at the movies when Edward G. Robinson or Jimmy Cagney mowed down the coppers with a Tommy Gun. The common denominator was an understanding of and an appreciation for the powerful potential of firearms.

These were guys who understood work – the manual labor kind – and knew their way around hammers, saws, wrenches and screwdrivers but they never looked at their weapons as simply tools for doing a job. You don't bet your life on a ball-peen hammer or a crescent wrench but you are making precisely that type of wager when you carry a weapon into close combat with an enemy just as determined and just as well-armed as you are. Army and Marine infantrymen – and to a different extent tankers, artillerymen and infantry support troops – understood that and developed a very personal relationship with their individual weapons. Often they took better care of those weapons than they did of themselves. Dirt and disease were unlikely to kill them but a dirty, malfunctioning weapon in a firefight most definitely would. Weapons maintenance in infantry units was a regular, monotonous chore but it was also a labor of love.

And the guys who souped-up Dad's tractor or built a rapid soapbox racer out of orange crates knew how to modify their weapons for better service. You'll see some of those field-expedient modifications in this book and it's a rare glimpse of American ingenuity. There are also some exceedingly rare photos of World War II infantry oddities such as the ill-fated Reising Submachine Gun, examples of which can be found at the bottom of Alligator Creek where most of the Marines who carried them into combat on Guadalcanal discarded them before the battle ended. And there are rare pictures of the UD M42 Marlin Submachine Gun that was issued to OSS Jedburg Teams operating behind German lines in Europe. It's rare, interesting stuff and the detail is extraordinary.

Author Tom Laemlein has done a spectacular job finding these rare photos but what I enjoy most is his keen eye in selecting shots that show the degree of comfort and reverence the World War II infantryman had felt about his weapons. For those of us who have carried some of these weapons into combat, it's fascinating, familiar and reassuring.

Grateful Appreciation

BY TOM LAEMLEIN

This book is the culmination of several years of photo collecting, research and learning. What began as a rather loose collection of several thousand wartime images has become a visual record of Americans in combat during World War II, a sort of still-frame documentary where the whole is greater than the sum of the parts. When you look at each image carefully, you will see something new and learn something new every time. I am grateful to Osprey Publishing for helping me produce this photo study and for joining with me in honoring America's fighting men of World War II.

Over the years I have purchased many technical books about US small arms from some of the most talented "gun writers" in the business. These same authors have been very supportive of my efforts to produce visual histories of the weapons, sharing their extensive knowledge and mentoring me in my research. It has been a remarkable experience, and goes to show how much can be achieved when people work together. I humbly thank Jim Ballou, Bruce Canfield, Dolf Goldsmith, Frank Iannamico, Edwin Libby, and Larry Ruth for their support and guidance. I am also quite proud that Captain Dale Dye provided the foreword for this book. Captain Dye and his team do stalwart work to make sure that many Hollywood film productions maintain a high level of historical accuracy.

Many thanks also go to Kate Moore, Rebecca Smart and John Tintera at Osprey Publishing for their vision and support of this project. The book's designer, Mike Gerenser, continues to set new standards in his craft by resurrecting World War II photography and bringing out the details in the images for all to see. Finally, I'd like to thank Jennifer Kelly, who patiently listens to all my stories about World War II weapons and endures countless hours at military museums and gun shows.

Enjoy the images and please remember to take a moment to pause and reflect on the sacrifices that were made for us in the cause of freedom by the veterans of World War II.

About the photographs: unless otherwise noted, the images in this book come from the United States National Archives, and the photo collection of the United States Marine Corps Historical Division.

Handguns

The American military has long had an affinity for handguns and during World War II the United States issued more pistols and revolvers than any other combatant nation. US handguns were normally only issued to officers, non-commissioned officers, and specialist troops (like tank crewmen). However, many frontline American troops found a way to equip themselves with a handgun in spite of issuance regulations, with many bartered for, borrowed, or outright stolen. Some pistols were brought along from home and many captured pistols were put to use for a soldier's self-defense long before they became treasured "war trophies".

There has been quite a bit of debate about the combat effectiveness of handguns and their relevancy on the battlefield. It is true that it is exceptionally difficult to shoot a pistol accurately at even short ranges under combat conditions. However, in the tight confines of a trench, inside a bunker, cave, or in room-to-room close combat, handguns have no equal. Another important factor is the morale-boost that a pistol gives an infantryman. Even if never used, the handgun gives the combat soldier some cold-steel comfort and in the right situation a vital competitive edge.

The most common American handgun during World War II was the M1911 or M1911A1 .45 caliber semi-automatic pistol. The M1911 was designed by John M. Browning, manufactured by Colt, and became endeared to American troops during World War I. A few small changes were made to the frame, trigger, hammer and grip and in 1926 the M1911 became the M1911A1. During World War II, more than 1.7 million M1911A1 pistols were manufactured by Colt, Remington-Rand, the Ithaca Gun Company and Union Switch & Signal.

The need for handguns in the US military increased dramatically after the attacks on Pearl Harbor in December 1941 and more than 180,000 M1917 Smith & Wesson and M1917 Colt .45 revolvers were brought back into service. These rugged veterans of World War I provided an able supplement while production of the M1911A1 ramped up. To further augment the supply of handguns, more than 250,000 Smith & Wesson "Victory Model" Revolvers (chambered in .38 Special) were manufactured. Most of the revolvers were issued to second-line troops, but these were effective weapons and some did find their way into combat. American handguns in World War II enjoyed a reputation for reliability and tremendous stopping-power with their massive .45 ammunition. The M1911A1 remained in US service until the 1980s, and there are many pistol enthusiasts who would prefer it to return as the standard American sidearm.

Left: The crew of "The Pay Off", a USMC M3 Stuart tank posing with their personal weapons on Bougainville. Included are three M1911A1 .45 caliber pistols, a M1A1 Thompson SMG, and one mean-looking machete.

A. A trooper of the 1st Cavalry cleans his Smith & Wesson M1917 .45 caliber revolver on the island of Los Negros during January 1944.
B. A Coast Guard shore patrolman poses with his Smith & Wesson M1917 .45 caliber revolver.

A. Marine crewmen of a M3 tank equipped with the Satan flame gun on Saipan during June 1944. The Marine at the left has a Smith & Wesson M1917 .45 caliber revolver in his shoulder holster, while the other crewman cradles a M1 Thompson SMG. **B.** A GI of the 36th Infantry Division, armed with a Smith & Wesson M1917 .45 caliber revolver, covers a surrendering German in Eastern France during September 1944. Note the large American flag patch on his sleeve and the captured German map case on his hip. **C.** A Marine armed with a .45 caliber M1917 revolver checks a bunker blasted open during the fighting on Okinawa during May 1945.

Armed with a Colt M1917 .45 revolver, a Marine cautiously makes his way past a Japanese casualty and into a cave on Okinawa.

A. A young Marine scout checks the body of a dead Japanese soldier on Okinawa. Note the M1911A1 .45 caliber pistol and the USMC Mark 2 "Kabar" fighting knife in the foreground. **B.** A Marine tanker armed with a M1911A1 .45 caliber pistol outside his disabled Sherman tank on Iwo Jima. The M1911A1 pistol was standard issue for AFV crews. **C.** Marine radio reporters on Iwo Jima in March 1945. Despite being a posed photo, there was always a real danger of enemy activity almost anywhere on that terrible little island.

A. A Marine demonstrates an unusual combat shooting stance with the M1911A1 .45 caliber pistol at a Pacific Training Center during October 1944.

B. Marines engaged in the deadly job of bunker and cave clearing on Okinawa during May 1945. The man on the right is armed with the M1 Garand rifle.

C. A crewman of the 631st Tank Destroyer Battalion uses the belly escape hatch of an M10 tank destroyer during training at Camp Shelby in May 1943.

The driver of a M3 Stuart light tank fires his M1911A1 pistol through his open visor during the Carolina war games, November 1941.

A. Men of the 23rd Infantry ("Americal Division") escort a Japanese prisoner to the rear on Bougainville during March 1944.
B. A GI of the 5th Army brings in a German prisoner at pistol point near Castleforte, Italy during May 1944.

A. Not all combat was with human enemies! An Air Corps crewman takes a four-legged prisoner with his M1911A1 .45 caliber pistol.
B. With a cine camera crew nearby, a Marine checks out a cave on Saipan in early July 1944.
C. Even while taking a break to brush their teeth these Marines keep a watchful eye out for Japanese infiltrators on Iwo Jima. Note the M1911A1 .45 caliber pistol in easy reach within a shoulder holster.

A GI investigates the wreck of a Afrika Korps command car near the Kasserine Pass, Tunisia during March 1943.

A. A Marine armed with the M1911A1 .45 caliber pistol moves up on Okinawa.

B. Men of the 84th Infantry Division interrogate a German civilian on the German border during January 1945.

A. Marines investigate the hidden entrance to a Japanese bunker/cave complex on Okinawa. Note that the hammer is cocked on the M1911A1 pistol.

B. Marines investigate a camouflaged "spider hole" on a Guadalcanal plantation.

C. Signs of a war to come: GIs investigate the entrance to a Japanese bunker beneath a thatched hut in India during 1944.

D. GIs inspect abandoned German grave markers outside St. Lô during August 1944. The man at the right is armed with a M1 Carbine.

Marine Raiders training with the M1911A1 .45 caliber pistol. Note that the man on the right has a privately-acquired hunting knife in a sheath.

A. A bazooka team of the 1st Marine Division on "Bloody Ridge" on the island of Peleliu during October 1944. The M1911A1 pistol was normally carried by heavy weapon crews for personal defense.
B. A tank destroyer crewman training with the M1911A1 .45 caliber pistol at Camp Hood Texas during 1943.

A. Marines prepare demolition charges to close up a large Japanese cave position on Okinawa. Note the M1911A1 .45 caliber pistol close at hand.

B. A GI armed with a M1911A1 pistol inside a bunker hollowed out of a hedgerow in Normandy during the summer of 1944.

C. A Signal Corps photographer carries a .45 caliber pistol as well as a camera on Makin Atoll during November 1943.

A Marine combat cinematographer armed with a M1911A1 .45 caliber pistol in the black volcanic ash of Iwo Jima, March 14, 1945.

A. A M1911A1 .45 caliber pistol used for a size-comparison photo next to a Japanese 150mm mortar shell captured on Peleliu.

B. A Marine flame gunner with a M1 flamethrower and a M1911A1 .45 caliber pistol. Saipan, June 1944.

C. Marines investigate a Japanese cave position on Tinian.

D. A GI inspects a Japanese coconut log and coral rock bunker at Munda, New Georgia during October 1943. These positions proved remarkably strong.

Thompson Submachine Gun

Many weapons are accepted for service and do their part to help a war effort in a workmanlike fashion. Others become more iconic, achieving technical "firsts" or receiving great praise and affection from the troops. Fewer still become the stuff of legends. Such is the case with the .45 caliber Thompson Submachine Gun (SMG).

Designed by John T. Thompson to serve as a "Trench Broom", the Thompson created a new category of military arms: the submachine gun. Too late for service in World War I, sales of the Thompson SMG stalled in the face of indifference (and greatly reduced budgets) of the American military during the 1920s. The Thompson gained some notoriety through its use by gangsters and G-Men during the late 1920s and through the early 1930s. Combat use of the Thompson SMG began with the Marines in Nicaragua and then in various incidents in China prior to World War II. After World War II began in Europe, orders for the Thompson SMG began to increase dramatically, and the US government sent many Thompson guns to England in 1940 under the Lend Lease Program.

The early variants of the Thompson SMG (the Model 1921 and Model 1928) were designed to accept either the 20 or 30-round "stick magazines" or the 50-round drum magazine. While the 50-round drum provided a tremendous amount of firepower, it was heavy, rattled, and was rather difficult to load. While the drum magazine faded quickly from US Army service, the Marines continued to use their drum magazines until the end of the war. The Thompson's .45 caliber slugs delivered man-stopping power at short range and the roar of the "Tommy Gun" often had an intimidating effect on the enemy.

Thompson guns were well crafted weapons and this fact was certainly appreciated by the troops. Allied troops began the war with finely made Thompson guns and were often suspicious and disdainful of later submachine guns (like the M3 Grease Gun and the Sten Gun) that were not made to the same standard. Even the wartime production M1 and M1A1 Thompson guns were well made and exceptionally reliable. Complaints about the Thompson came mostly at the strategic level as the guns were expensive and time consuming to produce. Objections from combat troops were focused on the Thompson's weight (at 10-plus pounds it was even heavier than the M1 Garand) and the short range of the .45 caliber ammunition.

In the eyes of the combat soldier the Thompson SMG became more than just an effective weapon, it was a legend in its own time. Until the worldwide proliferation of the AK-47, the Thompson was the iconic firearm associated with the term machine gun.

Left: Brothers in arms: Marine brothers photographed in action on Cape Gloucester during January 1944. The man to the left has a M1A1 Thompson SMG and his brother carries a M1 rifle.

A. A GI of the 148th Infantry Regiment fires his M1 Thompson SMG from a bunker on Bougainville during March 1943.
B. A Marine stands guard with a M1928 Thompson equipped with a 50-round drum magazine. Guadalcanal, early 1943.

This Marine believes in good-luck charms, and his M1928 Thompson gun is likely the most effective of them all. Okinawa, May 1945.

Two views of war dog handlers of the 2nd Marine Raiders on Bougainville during late 1943. Their M1928 Thompson guns have been field-modified with the addition of vertical handgrips.

A. A Marine Thompson gunner among the ruins on Saipan, June 1944.
B. A 5th Army GI playing a deadly game of cat-and-mouse with German snipers among the ruins of Cervare, Italy during January 1944.

A Marine armed with an M1A1 Thompson SMG defends his dugout position in the tropical rainforest of Cape Gloucester. The leatherneck to the lower right holds an M1 Carbine.

A. True combat photography is uncommon, but this grainy image shows a USMC Thompson gunner engaging Japanese troops less than 25 yards away on Peleliu in September 1944. Note that he wears the five-pocket magazine pouch for his Tommy Gun.

B. An early war GI shows off this M1928 Thompson gun. Note his M1917 helmet.

Marines armed with the M1A1 Thompson and the BAR fighting their way across the blasted landscape of Wana Ridge on Okinawa during May 1945.

A classic view of a Marine squad leader, armed with a M1A1 Thompson on Peleliu, October 1944.

A. German POWs pass an American tanker armed with a M1 Thompson SMG at Aachen, Germany in late October 1944.

B. Checking the papers of the local girls in Monschau, Germany during October 1944. This M1A1 Thompson has a field-modified metal reinforcing band on the weakly attached horizontal handgrip.

C. This Marine construction worker used his bulldozer and his M1A1 Thompson SMG to subdue a Japanese bunker and its defenders on Cape Gloucester in January 1944.

The Model 1928A1 Thompson in action with the Marines on Iwo Jima. This variant features a simplified ("L"-shaped) rear sight.

This GI has taped two 30-round magazines together for his M1 Thompson. This practice offered faster reloading and greater firepower, but conversely created an even heavier gun that was oddly unbalanced.

A. While the GI may not have been able to speak French particularly well, the Thompson gun opened the doors of friends and enemies alike.

B. A Marine with a M1928 Thompson SMG equipped with a 50-round drum, leads a patrol on Cape Gloucester in January 1944.

A. Firing the M1A1 Thompson at Japanese positions on Wana Ridge, Okinawa during May 1945.

B. A Marine combat cinematographer on Peleliu in September 1944. He is armed with an M1A1 Thompson SMG and probably needed it during this bloody Pacific battle.

C. Marines armed with the Thompson SMG on Okinawa in late May 1945. Note that the M1 Thompson in the background has been modified with a vertical handgrip.

Until the advent of the M3 SMG, the Thompson was standard issue for armored vehicle crews. This tank destroyer crewman shows off his M1928 at Camp Hood, Texas during 1943.

A. A GI with a M1A1 Thompson SMG and a captured Walther P-38 pistol keeps watch over two German POWs, Italy, April 1944.
B. An interesting image of a GI at the Tank Destroyer School at Camp Hood, Texas during 1943. His weapons include a M1928 Thompson as well as a "Molotov Cocktail".
C. A GI of the 87th Infantry Division waits for the word to move up. Germany, March 1945.

A. A Marine squad leader armed with a M1A1 Thompson during the bloody fighting on Peleliu in the fall of 1944.

B. A GI armed with a M1928 Thompson enjoys a phonograph captured from the Germans outside of Brest, France in August 1944.

C. Paratroopers of the 101st Airborne prepare for Operation *Market Garden* on September 17, 1944. The censor has partially obscured the patches on the paratrooper's sleeve.

Men of the 82nd Airborne Division have captured what will likely be their next meal in Normandy. The man on the left has a M1928 Thompson (as well as a M1911A1 .45 pistol in a shoulder holster) and the man to the right has a M1 Thompson. Note their neck scarves made from camouflage material.

A. A Signal Corps cinematographer in Algeria during December 1942. He carries an early M1928 Thompson with a vertical front handgrip. The vertical handgrips were somewhat fragile and prone to breakage.
B. A Tank Destroyer crewman demonstrates a low, sweeping firing stance with a M1928 Thompson Submachine Gun.

A trooper of the 113th Cavalry Regiment takes a break to have his portrait drawn. Note the M1928 Thompson and the details of the radio-command Jeep.

A. A barbershop with a tough clientele! A Marine gets a trim while cradling a M1928 Thompson with a 50-round drum magazine, while the barber is armed with a .45 caliber M1911A1 pistol. Guadalcanal, October 1942.

B. Marines in a hasty defensive position set up on Okinawa.

C. Men of the 442nd Infantry Regiment (Japanese-American troops) look over a wrecked SS halftrack in Italy. The man at the lower left of the image holds a M1 Thompson SMG.

A Marine on Guadalcanal keeps watch in a hilltop position with a M1928 Thompson equipped with a 50-round drum magazine. To his left is a five-pocket pouch for Thompson magazines. In the background is a Browning M1919A4 .30 caliber MG.

A GI armed with a M1 Thompson Submachine Gun examines potential intelligence taken from a German casualty in Brittany, August 1944.

Thompson gunners look over Japanese KIA in the China-Burma-India Theater during 1944.

A. A classic image of the Thompson Gun at war. This Marine, armed with an Model 1928 with a 50-round drum magazine (creating a nearly 15-pound gun) prowls the jungle of Cape Gloucester in January 1944. **B.** A Marine patrol passing through a jungle village on New Britain. The point man carries a M1928 Thompson with a 50-round drum magazine – a common USMC practice in the Southwest Pacific.
C. A Marine Thompson gunner escorts a Bazooka operator on Cape Gloucester.

A. Training with the M1929 Thompson at Camp Pendleton in July 1944. Note that there is no magazine in the gun.
B. Marines at New River, North Carolina wearing mix-and-match uniforms with camouflage veils. Their M1928 Thompson guns appear to be quite new.
C. Firing a M1A1 Thompson into a Japanese position on Cape Gloucester.

A. The .45 caliber Thompson was highly effective in the close confines of jungle combat. This M1 Thompson is seen with the Marines on Cape Gloucester in January 1944.
B. A fine portrait of a 3rd Armored Division GI armed with a M1 Thompson in France during August 1944. Note the metal reinforcing band that helps clamp the horizontal handgrip to the barrel.

The M1928A1 Thompson retained the removable butt stock feature. This Marine uses his M1928 without a butt stock as essentially a "machine pistol". Cape Gloucester, February 2, 1944.

A. A Marine armed with a M1928 Thompson during the Okinawa campaign. This weapon has the larger 30-round "stick magazine".

B. Marine paratroops dressed in early-war style jump suits and carrying M1928 Thompson SMGs. Marine paratroops ("Paramarines") later carried the folding wire-stock Reising Model 55 SMG.

C. A GI inside a covered dugout on the Schouten Islands during 1944. Note the M1918 "knuckle knife" in the foreground.

The Thompson Gun was not easy to fire from the low prone position as the bottom-mounted magazine projected down a bit too far, but it could be done, as evidenced by these photos.

A. A Thompson gunner guarding a road juncture already covered in anti-vehicle mines.

B. This Marine sergeant won the Navy Cross by wiping out several Japanese machine gun nests on Cape Gloucester. Obviously, he preferred the Thompson SMG. The M1 Thompson at the left has been modified with the addition of a vertical fore-grip.

M3 "Grease Gun"

In 1941 the United States was without a standardized submachine gun and the Thompson Model 1928 was only available in small numbers to American troops. Though the Thompson gun was a masterfully designed weapon and carefully crafted in production, it had two significant drawbacks. It was heavy (the Thompson Model 1928 weighed 10.8 pounds unloaded) and also expensive to produce. Before the war, a single Thompson gun cost the US Government as much as $209. As design changes created simplified versions, individual gun costs were first brought down to $70, and finally to $45 apiece in 1944. Even with the cost reductions, the Thompson was simply too expensive. Following the example set by the German MP40 and the British Sten Gun, US weapons designers began work on a submachine gun that was light and powerful, as well as quick and cost-effective to manufacture. The new design could be subcontracted out to small machine shops around the country for rapid manufacturing, and was the first American firearm to feature stamped and pressed metal, along with spot welding. Ingenious features included a telescoping wire frame butt stock (which could also be used as a cleaning rod). The M3 quickly earned the nickname "Grease Gun" for its resemblance to the mechanic's tool. Designated the US Submachine Gun .45 M3, the Grease Gun was chambered in the standard American pistol caliber (.45 ACP). It was accepted into US Army service on December 12, 1942, although it would be some time before the weapon would see combat. When finally approved for production, GM's Guide Lamp Division produced more than 600,000 M3 SMGs by the end of World War II. The M3 is a blowback weapon that fires from an open bolt and fires full automatic only. The low rate of fire (about 450 rounds per minute) makes the gun quite controllable and experienced shooters can easily obtain single shots. The M3 proved to be a robust, reliable and compact submachine gun. The advances in simplified production created a cost-effective weapon system, as each Grease Gun was estimated to cost less than $21. The M3 was originally intended as a "disposable" weapon, and troops were to throw it away when it ceased to work. However, in 1944 the limited supply of M3 SMGs forced US Army Ordnance workshops to fabricate various spare parts (which had never been created as part of the original low-cost concept of the M3) in order to keep the existing Grease Guns in operation.

Although it never completely replaced the Thompson SMG as planned, the M3 provided good service in World War II and soldiered on through the Korean War and into the early stages of the Vietnam War, and could still be found in the small arms racks of American armored vehicles into the mid 1990s.

Left: Demonstrating the M3 "Grease Gun" Submachine Gun during October 1944.

A. A Marine armed with the M3 SMG checking Japanese prisoners during the closing days of the fighting on Okinawa in 1945.
B. GIs of an armored infantry regiment pose with their M1 Carbine and M3 SMG during the drive into Germany during the spring of 1945.
C. An officer of the 7th Armored Division armed with a M3 SMG leads a foot patrol in the heavy snow outside Born, Belgium during January 1945.

A. The M3 Grease Gun with GIs of the 26th Infantry Division in Wiltz, Luxembourg during February 1945.

B. A M3-armed MP of the 36th Infantry Division towers over a tiny Wehrmacht soldier captured at Bruyeres, France in October 1944.

A. Men of the 69th Infantry Division enjoy the comforts of their home away from home. Germany, April 1945.

B. A trooper of the 325th Glider Infantry Regiment with the 82nd Airborne Division crouches near a captured German trailer with his M3 SMG. Belgium, January 1945.

C. An M3 with a member of the 167th Signal Company in October 1944. Taping several magazines together appears to have been a common practice, although it significantly increased the weight of the gun.

GIs of the 95th Infantry Division celebrate their unit's invasion of Germany. Note the man on the right wearing an SS dagger on his belt.

An M3-armed tanker of the 761st Tank Battalion ("Black Panthers") in France during late 1944. The folding stock Grease Gun was a handy replacement for Thompson SMG for vehicle crews.

A. A GI takes his M3 Grease Gun window shopping in Belgium in early 1945.
B. A GI test firing the M3 SMG in France during the late fall of 1944.

A. An entire story in one photo: Allied troops look over the body of a German soldier killed in a French church during September 1944. The man on the left is a Commonwealth soldier armed with a M1 Carbine. **B.** A GI of the 739th Tank Battalion watches the recovery of a Sherman Mine Exploder T1E3/M1 Roller. Note the "wood armor" attached to the side of the vehicle. The M3 SMG was becoming standard equipment for US tankers by late 1944.
C. A GI equipped with the "handie-talkie" portable radio and an M3 Grease Gun. Hurtgen Forest, November 1944.

A. Men of the 63rd Armored Infantry Battalion bring in German prisoners aboard a Jeep in Belgium during January 1945. Note that the Jeep is armed with a M1919A4 .30 caliber MG on a pedestal mount. **B.** Men of the 511th Parachute Infantry of the 11th Airborne Division pose with their weapons on Luzon, Philippines Islands during January 1945. **C.** An M3 Grease Gun during an early demonstration during June 1943. **D.** GIs of the 97th Infantry Division engaging snipers in Siegburg, Germany, April 10, 1945. The man with the slung M3 SMG also carries an M1 Carbine – a weapon which offers him greater range and accuracy.

A. The less comfortable aspects of the M3's collapsible wire stock are seen in this photo of an Ordnance officer demonstrating the Grease Gun during 1944.
B. A Jeep patrol in Brittany during August 1944. Note the 30-round magazine for the M3 SMG and the Mark II "Pineapple" fragmentation grenades.
C. A patrol of the US 7th Army along the Siegfried Line. Note that each M3 has two magazines taped together.

A. A MP of the 1st Infantry Division shows the M3 SMG to men of the newly re-formed Belgian Army in September 1944.
B. A photo for the folks back home: a GI posing with his M3 SMG in a training camp.

The M3 is demonstrated to troops in the field. Burma, November 1944.

A. The M3 during initial testing. The relatively low cyclic rate allows for easily controlled automatic firing. Note the three spent casings exiting the ejection port.
B. GIs of the 81st Infantry Division among the ruins of Palau Island in September 1944. This would be among the earliest appearances of the M3 SMG in Pacific combat.
C. GIs observe Coast Guard anti-aircraft gunners during their voyage across the North Atlantic.

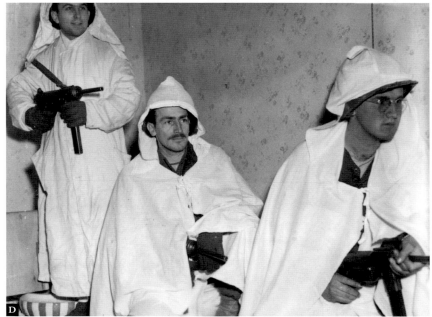

A. American officers interview Belgian civilians to obtain local intelligence on German troop movements.

B. A paratrooper of the 17th Airborne Division guards young German prisoners with his M3 "Grease Gun". Germany, April 1944.

C. Men of the 14th Armored Division use their M3 SMGs to blast open the lock to the main gate of Hammelburg Prison.

D. Camouflaged with snow capes, this M3-armed patrol of the 104th Infantry Division prepares for a mission in the Roer River area during early March 1945.

A patrol of the 75th Infantry Division in the Ardennes during late December, 1944. The "Grease Gun" was much lighter and easier to carry than the Thompson SMG.

Reising Submachine Gun

The Reising Submachine Gun is likely one of the least known, and consequently most misunderstood weapons in the US arsenal of World War II. The gun's inventor, Eugene G. Reising, saw an opportunity to capitalize on the rapidly growing arms industry by developing a submachine gun design. Reising contracted with the arms firm of Harrington & Richardson to produce his SMG, and production of the Reising Model 50 SMG began at Harrington & Richardson in December, 1941. Timing worked in his favor as America entered World War II during that same month and the US military was caught without enough submachine guns to meet the new demand. The Reising was tested by both the US Army and by the Marine Corps, but only the USMC accepted the Reising for service. Even so, the Marine Corps only accepted the Reising as a supplemental weapon until enough Thompson SMGs became available.

Among the Reising's inherent problems was the overall unreliability of its 20-round magazine, with flimsy feed lips that were easily bent which lead to frequent jamming. The small magazine capacity was also quickly exhausted by the Reising's fast cyclic rate. The Reising also required lubricating oil to function properly and this attracted more dirt and grime that would foul the action. These factors coupled with the harsh jungle conditions of the Solomon Islands made the Reising an unpopular weapon with the Marines.

Two versions of the Reising SMG were used during World War II. The initial version was the Model 50, which was chambered for the standard .45 ACP cartridge, fitted with a full size wooden stock with sling swivels, and equipped with a compensator at the end of the barrel. Metal cooling fins extended a third of the way down the barrel from the receiver. The second version, the Model 55, was developed for use with new Paramarine (Marine paratroops) units. The Model 55 was a significantly shortened gun, featuring a folding metal "wire stock" and a pistol grip stock. The compensator was eliminated to save length and weight, but in all other respects the modified gun was the same as the Model 50. As the Marines ultimately did not use paratroop units, the Reising Model 55 guns were issued to Marine Raiders and other specialized troops. The Model 55's wire shoulder stock was rather flimsy and many times the wire stocks were discarded and the guns used as a machine pistol.

Delivery of Reising SMGs to the Marine Corps was finished in early 1943, and by the end of that year the gun was no longer listed on USMC equipment rolls. The exact number of Reising SMGs produced by Harrington & Richardson is not known. Researchers estimate that up to 100,000 of the guns were made, but this would include all civilian variants and guns provided to Allied nations. The Marine contract called for 65,000 Reising guns of all types but it is unlikely that the full order was procured. The remainder of the Reisings did their duty guarding war plants and prisons, as well as shipboard duty in the US Navy and Coast Guard.

Left: The Reising Model 55 Submachine Gun. The Model 55 is the folding stock version of the SMG, specially designed for the Paramarines, USMC parachute troops. Note the Marine's padded jump uniform.

Both models of the Reising SMG with Marines during the early days of the Guadalcanal operation in 1942. On the far left is the folding stock Model 55, in the center is full stock Model 50, and in the background is a BAR.

The tools of the trade for Marine Raiders: the Reising Model 55 and Model 50 sandwiched between the M1928 Thompson SMG (top) and the Colt M1911A .45 caliber pistol and M1 Carbine (bottom).

A. Marine Raiders dressed in "frogskin" camouflage uniforms take cover during a beach landing in the Solomon Islands. The man in the foreground is armed with a Reising Model 55 (with its muzzle pointing up).   **B.** Marine Raiders on Guadalcanal armed with the Reising Model 55 Submachine Gun.
C. A Coast Guard shore patrol shows off its firepower with Reising Model 50 SMGs and Stevens Model 520-30 Trench Guns.
D. USMC "Navajo Code Talkers" equipped with a Reising Model 55 SMG. This was at the end of the Reising's field service life with the Marine Corps.

Marine Raiders, all Texans, pose with their Reising Model 55 SMGs on Guadalcanal.

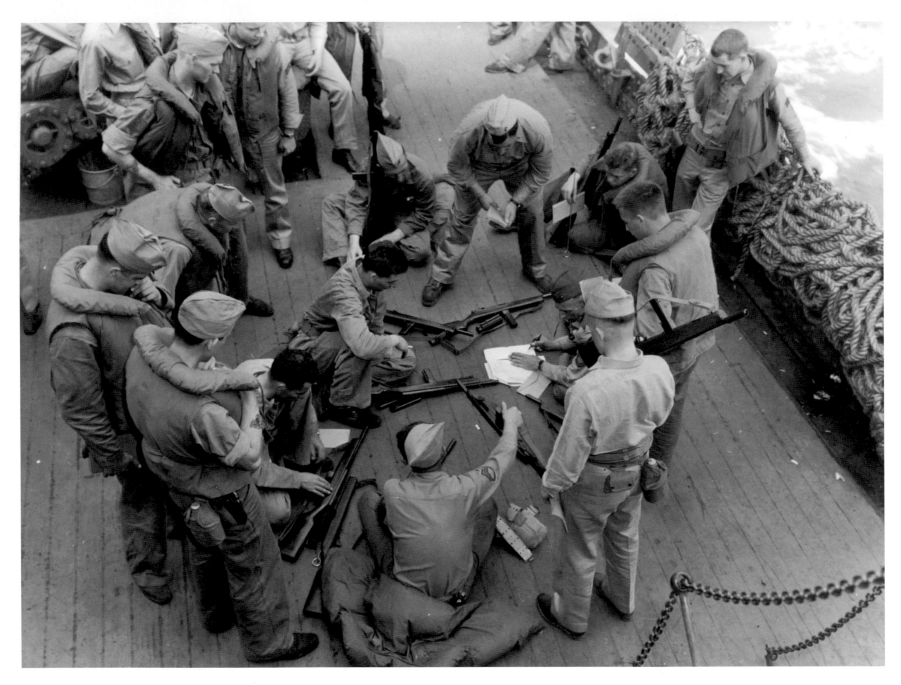

Next stop Guadalcanal. Marines familiarize themselves with the Reising Model 50 SMG on their way to the Solomon Islands during early August, 1942.

A & B. Marines with both models of the Reising SMG at the New River Training Center during August 1942.

C. Essential cleaning: A Marine Sergeant wipes down his Reising Model 55, "somewhere in the Pacific" during February 1943.

D. Marine instructors on the ranges at Quantico, testing the Reising Model 55 in 1941. Note the man on the left has a Thompson M1928 Submachine Gun.

Paramarines pose in their camouflage jump gear with folding stock Reising Model 55 SMGs during training in Southern California, February 1943.

A. A Marine Corps signalman with a Reising Model 50 during airbase security exercises.
B. A Marine sentry with his "Devil Dog", armed with the Reising Model 55. The stateside police and guard duty environment was where the Reising SMG proved most successful.

Marine Raiders armed with both the Reising Model 50 and Model 55 (as well as the Springfield M1903 rifle) display trophies captured on New Guinea in early 1943.

Marines loading onto transports in San Francisco, bound for the Solomon Islands. Several of the men are armed with the Model 55. Note the man at the far right has a small cine camera.

A. USMC combat cameraman armed with the Reising Model 55. Bougainville, November 1943.
B. Off-hand firing of the Reising Model 55 at Quantico in early 1942. The flimsy wire stock did not provide a comfortable shooting platform.
C. A Marine recruit learns to fire the Reising Model 50. Parris Island, September 1942.
D. Firing the folding stock Model 55. The feed lips on the Reising magazines were delicate and it is ultimately inadvisable to grasp the magazine and use it as a fore-grip.

A. Training at New River in September 1943, this Marine has a hodgepodge of equipment, including a Reising Model 50 SMG and a M1917 bayonet.
B. The Reising SMG joins the Corps: A Marine Master Gunnery Sergeant displays the Model 55 and Model 50 at Quantico in early 1942.

UD M42 Marlin Submachine Gun

The UD M42 Submachine Gun is a virtually unknown weapon in America's World War II arsenal. As war clouds loomed on the horizon for America in 1939-1941 several submachine gun designs were developed by American gun companies. The patents for what became the UD M42 were originally assigned to the High Standard Manufacturing Company but no orders were obtained from the American military or any foreign army. Eventually the rights to manufacture the guns were turned over to the United Defense Supply Corporation and were produced at the Marlin Firearms Company of New Haven, CT.

The UD M42, as finally constructed by Marlin Firearms, was finely made of milled steel. The UD M42 was chambered in either .45 ACP or 9mm, and featured a curious dual 20-round magazine set up. After one magazine was finished the entire magazine assembly (of two magazines) would be rotated to insert the second 20-round magazine into the weapon. Eventually, the Dutch government ordered 15,000 UD M42 guns chambered in 9mm but these were never delivered before the Japanese conquest of the Dutch East Indies. The Office of Strategic Services (OSS), the forerunner of the CIA, used more than 14,000 of the UD M42s in operations around the globe and also in cooperation with the British Special Operations Executive (SOE). OSS operatives are known to have used the UD M42 in combat in France, the Balkans, the Mediterranean, and in the China-Burma-India sector. Reports about the guns revealed that they were very well made and were considered reliable and accurate in field use.

Made of machined steel and using no stamped parts whatsoever, the UD M42 was very expensive to manufacture. As the American military was focused on cost-effective, mass-produced weapons systems, the UD M42 quickly disappeared from the US service. Despite its lack of celebrity, the UD M42 is one of the finest submachine guns ever built and an important weapon in America's World War II arsenal. Unfortunately, as OSS operations were secret, photos of the UD M42 Submachine Gun in service are very rare. We are happy to publish some very rare views of this gun in combat.

Left: A wounded OSS agent armed with a UD M42 photographed outside Langres, France with US infantry in 1944. This man was probably a part of one of the Jedburgh missions to gather intelligence for the US Army.

A. A large group of UD M42 submachine guns set to be distributed to Greek partisans by OSS agents during 1944. *(Via Osprey Publishing)*
B. An OSS agent of "Detachment 101" armed with a UD M42 in the hills of Burma. *(Via Osprey Publishing)*   **C.** OSS agents of Operational Group "Alice" in Southern France aboard locally procured transport during 1944. The UD M42 submachine gun is in evidence along with a Bazooka strapped to the cab of the truck. *(Via Osprey Publishing)*
D. An OSS agent (second from left) armed with a UD M42, with French Resistance fighters in Central France during the summer of 1944. *(Via Osprey Publishing)*

OSS agents operating in the Balkans pose with their UD M42 submachine guns. *(Via Frank Iannamico)*

M1 Carbine

During World War II the M1 Carbine represented a new class of battlefield weapon, originally defined as a "Light Rifle". Ultimately the M1 Carbine has become one of the most beloved and yet often completely misunderstood weapons in the American arsenal during World War II.

The Carbine was designed to provide troops that were normally armed with pistols or submachine guns (for example: paratroops, communications men, artillery and armor crews) with a light, handy rifle that delivered sufficient short-range firepower. Compared to the .45 caliber M1911A1 pistol and Thompson Submachine Gun the M1 Carbine is much easier to use and much more accurate (easily effective at 100 yards). The Carbine quickly became a favorite of troops across the board – light, handy and very easy to shoot.

Accepted into US service as the "Carbine, Caliber .30 M1", the M1 Carbine was a Winchester concept that won the Ordnance Department design competition beginning in September 1941. Interestingly, Carbine manufacturing during World War II never took place at Springfield Arsenal, instead production was distributed among ten different manufacturing firms: Winchester Repeating Arms, Inland Manufacturing Division of General Motors, Underwood-Elliot-Fisher, Rock-Ola Manufacturing, Quality Hardware Machinery Corporation, National Postal Meter, Irwin-Pedersen Arms Company, Standard Products, International Business Machines, and Saginaw Steering Gear Division of General Motors. Production of the M1 Carbine exceeded all expectations and the weapon was even considered over-produced by Ordnance standards with more than 6.2 million M1 Carbines (including the folding stock variant, the M1A1) built before the end of the war.

Despite its tremendous popularity, the M1 Carbine presented a couple of notable problems. It was chambered for a wholly new cartridge – the .30 Carbine and while the Carbine shared the same bore size as the M1 and M1903 rifles, the Carbine's ammunition was little more powerful than a pistol round. Initial logistical problems were easily overcome, but the deficiencies in man-stopping power with the Carbine were never overcome. The best way to assess the M1 Carbine is put in proper context—as a replacement weapon for the M1911A1 pistol and Thompson Submachine Gun. It was never intended to replace, or even supplement, the M1 Garand as a battle rifle.

The M1 Carbine is exceptionally "collectible" among American gun buyers. There are a couple of items that cause some confusion among novice collectors and casual observers. Although many M1 Carbines are now found with a bayonet lug, these were added after World War II. The same is true for widened (sometimes called "pot belly") stocks to accommodate the M2 conversion kit which gave the Carbine selective-fire capability (full automatic or semi-automatic). The select-fire M2 Carbine and its 30-round magazine were also not issued in World War II. The extensive post war arsenal rebuild program brought back standard configuration M1 Carbines and replaced worn out parts, also adding new parts which included bayonet lugs, flip safeties, adjustable rear sights, and in many cases converted the guns into M2 selective-fire weapons.

Left: A Marine Raider poses with his M1 Carbine on New Georgia. The light, handy Carbine quickly became a favorite of American troops in every combat theater.

A. A GI of the 30th Infantry Division carrying an M1 Carbine equipped with a stock pouch (which contains two 15-round magazines). August 15, 1944.
B. USMC flamethrower instructors pose with the tools of their trade, the M1 flamethrower and the M1 Carbine. Australia, July 1943.
C. A Marine cradles his M1 Carbine while he takes a break on Cape Gloucester.

Worn down from a long day of marching, a GI with a M1 Carbine adopts a pose shared by all tired infantrymen, including the World War I statue behind him. Italy 1944.

A GI of the 6th Armored Division looks over a captured German "listening post" outside Brest, France on August 30, 1944. This man wears a captured German bayonet.

A GI enjoys a toast to victory in France during the summer of 1944. His M1 Carbine is equipped with a stock pouch for two extra magazines and a M8 grenade launcher.

A. Men of the 2nd Armored Division outside a bunker in France, October 1944. They have created a small "sidewalk" using packing tubes for artillery ammunition.

B. Marines armed with the M1 Carbine and Thompson submachine gun on Cape Gloucester during January 1944.

C. Men of the 12th Armored Division unload an M3 halftrack that has hit a mine at Bining, France during early December 1944. The M1 Carbine was standard equipment for many vehicle crews.

Battle-weary GIs in the streets of Bastogne during the Battle of the Bulge. The man at left carries an M1 Carbine fitted with a stock pouch.

A. A 5th Army GI in action with an M1 Carbine at Cisterna, Italy during May 1944.
B. On the northern front of the Bulge, a GI of the 99th Infantry Division emerges from a bunker with his M1 Carbine.

The last days of the Reich: GIs of the 11th Armored Division fire on German holdouts near Kepple, Austria in early May, 1945.

A. A Marine war dog handler armed with an M1 Carbine on Iwo Jima. This dog is likely a messenger, carrying orders, medical supplies and ammunition to Marines isolated on the battlefield.

B. A Marine on Okinawa with girls on his mind and his M1 Carbine close by.

C. A GI in Western Europe with his two best friends.

A. Marine flame gunner on Okinawa equipped with the M2 flamethrower and the M1 Carbine for personal defense.
B. A member of the 66th Signal Company entertains his fellow GIs at Eisenbach, Germany in April 1945. His M1 Carbine and a holstered M1911A1 .45 caliber pistol are within easy reach.
C. A Marine engaging Japanese troops at close range with an M1 Carbine. Okinawa, 1945.

A. A radio operator at work inside an M3 command halftrack in Northern France, fall 1944.

B. A Lieutenant of the 45th Infantry Division using a "handie-talkie" radio in the ruins of a German town, March 1945. Note the fighting knife on his belt and the stock pouch on his M1 Carbine.

C. This young Marine, hardened by weeks of hard fighting on Peleliu, poses with his M1 Carbine during October 1944.

A. A Marine radio operator at work on Iwo Jima.

B. A trooper of the 10th Armored Division shares a smoke with a Belgian policeman in January 1945.

C. A Ranger reloads the 15-round magazine to his M1 Carbine on Omaha Beach.

A. A Marine of the 6th Marine Division armed with a M1 Carbine overlooking the outskirts of Naha, Okinawa.

B. A trooper of the 113th Cavalry Regiment examines the rockets from a German 21cm Nebelwerfer 42, in Germany during April 1945. Cavalry units were extensively equipped with the M1 Carbine.

C. Marines armed with M1 Carbines investigate a large cave on Okinawa.

Marines examine a Japanese 150mm shell on Okinawa. The man at left holds an M1 Carbine fitted with a stock pouch. Note the Marine at center has a customized holster for his .45 caliber M1911A1 pistol.

Recon patrol: A GI scouts for the advance of the 79th Infantry Division in Germany during January 1945.

Marines on Cape Gloucester armed with a wide variety of weapons. The man at left has an M1 Carbine and a .45 caliber M1911A1 pistol. The man at right has a M1A1 Thompson SMG. In the foreground is a Czech-made ZB26 light machine gun captured from the Japanese.

A Marine officer armed with an M1 Carbine calls in naval fire support for his beachhead position during the invasion of Peleliu.

A combat cinematographer of 165th Signal Company with his cine camera and an M1 Carbine. France 1944.

Freedom of religion: a young Marine takes Holy Communion on the stark landscape of Iwo Jima during the fighting there in 1945.

A Marine cleans his M1 Carbine on Iwo Jima. Note the stock pouch attached to the butt.

Winning hearts and minds: a GI of the 31st Infantry Division meets with natives on Morotai Island (Indonesia) during the late fall of 1944. Note his M1 Carbine equipped with a stock pouch.

A Marine checks the entrance to a Japanese bunker/cave on Okinawa.

M1903 Springfield Rifle

The M1903 Springfield rifle is the classic American bolt action rifle which is best remembered for its service in the hands of the Doughboys of the American Expeditionary Force (AEF) in the trenches of World War I, and less so for its contributions during World War II. In actuality, the .30 caliber Springfield was the less-used rifle in World War I (that honor going to the M1917 Enfield), while serving longer and in much greater numbers during World War II.

It took until the early months of 1943 before the M1 Garand rifle began to replace the Springfield in Marine Corps service. The Marines used the venerable Springfield throughout the fighting on Guadalcanal and well into the Solomon Islands campaign. Army units used the Springfield rifle in the desperate fighting in the Philippines during late 1941 and early 1942. The Springfield was also the primary rifle for many Army troops in North Africa, Sicily and into the Italian campaign.

Photos show the Springfield interspersed with the M1 rifle in Army units in Italy until late in 1943. Even in Western Europe the Springfield was commonly found, often used as a grenade-launching rifle by frontline troops. Many GIs preferred the Springfield's lighter weight as compared to the M1 rifle. The Springfield rifle equipped with the M1 grenade launcher was commonplace in Army units, and many remained in service as a "grenade launching specialty rifle" after M1 Garand rifles had been issued to that unit. One of the primary reasons for the M1903 rifles remaining in service so long is because the M1 grenade launcher could be fitted to a bolt-action Springfield without interrupting its ability to fire normally.

The Springfield also played a strong role in training, and the use of Springfield rifles with training units allowed more M1 rifles to be sent to troops overseas. The Springfield rifle also provided US troops with their standard sniper rifle in World War II. The Ordnance Department used the simplified (for wartime production) M1903A3 rifle to create the M1903A4 (sniper), equipped with a telescopic sight. The Marine Corps used modified "national match" edition Springfield rifles as sniper rifles, and also used the earlier M1903A1 as the basis for their M1903A1/Unertl sniper rifle.

The M1903 Springfield was finally declared obsolete in 1947, ending the career of one of the greatest battle rifles in history. Today Springfield rifles are very popular on the collector market, and many examples of World War II produced rifles can be found. These highly accurate veterans of two world wars will still be found on rifle ranges for years to come.

Left: Evoking a vision of the defenders of Wake Island, this soldier takes aim with his M1903 Springfield equipped with a M1905 16-inch bayonet.

A. In the dark days of early 1942 American troops deployed into beachside positions in anticipation of a potential Axis invasion. This soldier is armed with the .30 caliber M1903 Springfield rifle.

B. A GI in training using a .30 caliber cartridge box as a rifle rest for his M1903 Springfield.

C. A soldier armed with a M1903 Springfield at Fort Story, Virginia during March 1942. He wears the World War I–vintage M1917 helmet.

A. Posing for what would become a famous recruiting poster for the USMC, this man carries the M1903 Springfield rifle with a M1905 bayonet, and wears the M1917 helmet.
B. Army Air Corps troops armed with the M1903 Springfield rifle while stationed in Alaska during 1942.

The M1903 Springfield rifle ready to defend America in early 1942.

A. Brigadier General Benjamin O. Davis inspects a M1903 Springfield rifle in England during August 1942.

B. The rare M1903 Springfield "Bushmaster" carbine – a M1903 rifle with its barrel cut down to 18 inches. The "Bushmaster" was created by the 158th Infantry Regiment while stationed in the Panama Canal Zone.

C. A paratrooper of the 101st Airborne carries a M1903 Springfield set up as a grenade launching rifle during Operation *Market Garden* in Holland, September 18, 1944.

A. Navy Seabees training with the M1903 Springfield rifle during 1943.
B. Easy duty! A GI armed with a M1903 Springfield rifle gets a cup of coffee from a Dutch girl while guarding a barge near Antwerp during February 1945.

A Marine carrying a M1903A3 (World War II production) rifle examines a Japanese dugout on Bougainville, December 1943.

A sniper of the 36th Infantry Division cleans his M1903A4 sniper rifle in Italy during May 1944. Note that even at this late date that most of the GIs in this unit are armed with Springfield rifles.

The M1903 Springfield saw extensive service as a grenade launching rifle. This example is seen with the M1 grenade launcher and the M9A1 anti-tank grenade.

A. A detail view of the M1 grenade launcher mounted on the M1903 Springfield rifle. The raised rings on the launcher were used to set the range on the rifle grenade.
B. The Springfield remained as the primary battle rifle for the USMC until well into 1943. This Marine rifleman still carries a Springfield on Guam in September 1944.

A Marine sniper team armed with a M1903A1 sniper rifles (equipped with the Unertl scope) in action on Okinawa during May 1945.

A Marine makes notes on Japanese aerial activity over Russell Island during August 1943.

"Muleskinners" of the 504th Parachute Infantry Battalion armed with the M1903 Springfield rifle. The machine gun strapped to the mule is a Browning M1919A4. Venafro, Italy December 1943.

Army troops using a Springfield M1903A3 rifle (foreground) and a M1903A4 sniper rifle (background) in Burma during January 1945. Fragmentation grenades set up for use as rifle grenades can be seen on the ground ahead of the shooters.

Communications troops stringing wire in France during the summer of 1944. Note that the corporal on the left is armed with a M1903 Springfield rifle as well as a M1 Carbine.

A Marine sniper with a M1903A1/Unertl rifle. This combination of the Springfield with the Unertl scope was the most effective USMC sniper rifle of World War II.

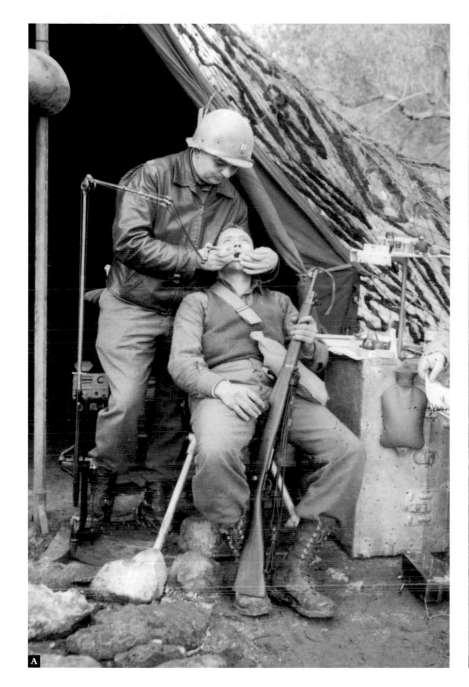

A. Field dentistry outside Capriati, Italy with the 57th Signal Battalion during December 1943. Is the M1903 Springfield rifle there to protect the patient against the Germans or the dentist?

B. The M1903 Springfield seen during field exercises at the Desert Training Center during September 1942.

An MP armed with a M1903A3 rifle checks the papers of Belgian refugees near the critical road juncture at Bastogne, December 11, 1944 – less than ten days prior to the German attacks during the Battle of the Bulge.

Marines working with Guadalcanal locals in late 1942. Note the M1903 Springfield rifle and the local's cutlass!

M1917 Enfield Rifle

The M1917 rifle was America's unsung hero of World War I. The rifle was a slight modification of the British Pattern 1914 rifle, re-chambered in the US 30 caliber. Officially called the Model of 1917, many Americans refer to it as the "Enfield". The M1917 rifles were manufactured by Winchester, Remington and Eddystone (a Remington subsidiary). During World War I, the majority of troops in the American Expeditionary Force were armed with the M1917. While not as attractive as the M1903 Springfield rifle, the M1917 was a robust and effective battle rifle, equipped with excellent sights. After World War I, existing stocks of the M1917 were retained in reserve.

When the United States was suddenly thrust into World War II in December 1941, the American military faced a severe shortage of rifles. The M1917s were brought out of storage and refurbished at various American arsenals. Several thousand M1917s were sent to England as part of the Lend-Lease Program and were used by British Home Guard units. Thousands more had been sent to the Philippines and even more were provided to the Nationalist Chinese Army.

As a battle rifle, the M1917 is a highly accurate, robust and reliable weapon. The M1917's adjustable rear sight is in many ways superior to the sights on the M1903 Springfield rifle. While the M1917 was never derided, it was certainly never celebrated. The Springfield rifle and the later M1 Garand captured all the attention as America's battle rifles.

The M1917 trained many American troops, providing a large number of men with their first experience in handling a firearm. While few M1917s made it into combat with American forces during World War II, many of these rifles were issued to artillery, communication and other troops stationed just behind the front lines. The M1917 was declared obsolete soon after the end of World War II, bringing to a close the career of an effective but often overlooked weapon.

In the current collector's market, the M1917 is gaining popularity and value as a new generation of American rifle shooters learn what a fine firearm it is. On the rifle range it is the equal of any contemporary bolt-action rifle.

Left: Training for action: a new recruit on a combat exercise with a .30 caliber M1917 Enfield rifle.

A. A rare image of the M1917 Enfield in combat in World War II.

B. A Moroccan soldier of the multi-national force guarding German prisoners in Italy during January 1944. The M1917 rifle was provided to several Allied nations.

C. Large numbers of the M1917 were provided to the Nationalist Chinese Army. This example is seen in service with the Chinese 38th Division in action in Burma during February 1944.

A. The M1917 in bayonet practice at Camp Robinson during July 1942.

B. The M1917 rifle with the M1917 bayonet during 1942. This weapon trained many American recruits in the early war period.

C. Chinese troops with the M1917 Enfield rifle combine bayonet training with hand-fighting martial arts.

D. A soldier of the 4th French Moroccan Division armed with a M1917 Enfield rifle at Mulhouse France, November 22, 1944.

A. Troops of the newly reformed Dutch Army in action with the M1917 Enfield rifle during November 1944.

B. Hand to hand combat training with the 807th Tank Destroyer Battalion at Camp Gruber during 1943.

C. Rifle training at Camp Williams, Utah during 1942. Even though considered a second-line weapon in US service, the M1917 was a fine battle rifle.

D. New recruits see the raw brutality of combat on the bayonet course.

A. A member of the 23rd Infantry "Americal" Division armed with a M1917 configured as a sniper rifle. This is an unidentified modification and may be a "one-off".

B, C & D. Army troops training with the M1917 Enfield rifle wearing the herringbone twill (HBT) camouflage suit and nets.

M1 Garand Rifle

The United States Rifle, Caliber .30, M1 has become known by several names. It is often called "the Garand" after its inventor John C. Garand, or more simply the M1. General George S. Patton called the M1 rifle "the greatest battle implement ever devised". In the final accounting, General Patton's statement may provide the most apt description of this remarkable weapon.

The semi-automatic M1 replaced the bolt-action M1903 Springfield as the standard battle rifle of the US Army in 1936 (the USMC adopted the M1 in late 1941) with production beginning in 1937. This represented quite an advance in infantry weapons as the M1 was the first semi-automatic rifle to be adopted by any army. After the M1's gas port system was modified in 1940, the rifle remained in production, unchanged, until 1957 and serving through the Korean War and into the Vietnam War. Before World War II came to an end, more than 4 million M1 rifles were produced at the Springfield Armory and Winchester Repeating Arms (where a little more than 500,000 were made).

The M1 had its share of teething issues and faced serious opposition from many "old salts" in the US military. Initial reactions were not positive as the M1 represented new technology and many experienced riflemen preferred the traditional bolt-action Springfield rifle (the loss of an "expert" marksman rating would cost a soldier almost 15 percent of his pay). The M1 is heavier than the Springfield and there were concerns about ammunition jamming with the new semi-automatic rifle. Once US troops entered combat in World War II these concerns quickly disappeared when the increased firepower of the M1 made itself apparent.

The M1 features a unique internal magazine that is fed by 8-round chargers (or "clips"). While the rifle cannot be "topped off", it is very quick and easy to reload. World War II saw the transition to an era of rapid firepower, and the M1 rifle gave American infantrymen a tremendous advantage on the battlefield. The M1 proved to be incredibly robust, reliable and accurate, performing without equal on the World War II battlefield. Many GIs owe their lives to John Garand's rifle while many of Germany and Japan's best infantrymen fell in a storm of .30 caliber fire from the M1.

Today the M1 Garand is much in demand with American gun collectors and target shooters. Through the good work of the Civilian Marksmanship Program, tens of thousands of M1s remain ready for action in private hands, now sending lead down range at paper targets instead of Axis infantry.

Left: Photographed for an Army recruiting poster in 1942, this soldier shows off the "new" M1 rifle while still wearing the World War I vintage M1917 helmet.

A. A paratrooper of the 1st Airborne Task Force with his M1 rifle mounting an M1 bayonet (with a 10-inch blade). Southern France, August 1944. Note the ammunition bandolier around his waist.
B. A GI of the 4th Infantry Division with an M1 rifle outside his earth and log bunker in Northern France, October 1944.
C. A mortar man of the 42nd Infantry Division loaded down with 81mm mortar shells and his M1 rifle. Australia, December 1942.

Sharpshooters of the 75th Infantry Division reloading their M1 rifles on the rooftop of a Belgian farmhouse during December 1944.

A. The M1 rifle did deadly work. A GI of the 83rd Infantry Division reloads his M1 near German casualties outside of Houffalize, Belgium during the Battle of the Bulge.
B. GIs of the 94th Infantry Division fire across the Rhine River near Mannheim with an M1 rifle and a BAR (background) during March 1945.
C. An M1-armed rifleman of the 30th Infantry Division looks over a German casualty on the road to St. Lo, France in early July 1944.

A. Men of the 84th Infantry Division searching German civilians at Krefeld, Germany in March 1945. Note the size of the M1 rifle compared to the relatively short GI carrying it.
B. A Bazooka gunner's assistant carrying a full load of 2.36-inch rockets as well as his M1 rifle. Italy 1944.

A. The M1 rifle was easy to load quickly even in the heat of combat. This Marine inserts an 8-round clip of .30 caliber ammunition into his M1 on Bougainville.

B. Army recruits learn to use the M1 rifle at Fort Benning in 1943. Note the use of the sling to help create a tripod-like position for the shooter in the prone position.

C. A Marine in "frogskin" camouflage fires his M1 rifle at Japanese snipers on Cape Gloucester in December 1943. The powerful .30-06 ammunition could easily penetrate jungle foliage to reach its target.

A rifleman of the 37th Infantry Division engages Japanese targets with his M1 in the Philippines during June 1945. Note the bandolier around his chest, holding multiple 8-round clips for his M1.

The normal look of the American rifleman in Germany during the winter of 1945: M1 rifle, fatigue jacket, boots and ammo bandoliers. 80th Infantry Division, March 1945.

A. GIs of the 79th Infantry Division take advantage of prefabricated concrete bunkers captured from the Germans. Dinslaken, Germany on March 30, 1945.

B. Troops remove a dead Japanese soldier from a culvert on Leyte, December 22, 1944.

C. The M1 is a remarkably accurate weapon. Here a GI of the 30th Infantry Division targets German snipers with the help of Belgian resistance fighters, September 11, 1944.

D. American troops gather around a Luftwaffe bomber crewman who perished after his aircraft was shot down over Iceland. April 23, 1943.

A. Marines firing on Japanese troops on Iwo Jima. The Marine at the far right uses an M1 Carbine, while his partners carry the M1 rifle. The two weapons became interwoven in combat units after 1943.

B. The M1 deployed into combat early with US Army units. This group of M1 rifles is seen at Dutch Harbor, Alaska during October 1942.

C. In advanced training at Camp Hood during 1943, this GI of the 102nd Infantry Division carries an M1 rifle mounting the M1905 bayonet with a 16-inch blade.

A classic image of a Marine rifleman and his M1 Garand.

The M1 in action with the "Band of Brothers" of the 101st Airborne on "the island" (between the Lower Rhine and the Waal River) Holland, November 1, 1944. Note the cartridge and clip ejected from the rifle at right.

A Marine photographed "somewhere in the South Pacific" with his M1 rifle equipped with the long-blade M1905 bayonet.

A. A Marine firing a rifle grenade with his M1 rifle equipped with a M7 grenade launcher. The M7 launcher would not allow the rifle to be fired in its normal semi-automatic mode.
B. Shades of World War I: A GI fires his M1 from a trench on the Western Front in France 1944.

A young Marine demonstrates the proper prone firing position with his M1 rifle.

A. A Marine firing his M1 into a Japanese log bunker on Cape Gloucester.

B. Breaching the Siegfried Line: A GI of the 65th Infantry Division points to a massive armor plate of a demolished German bunker. Powerful though it was, his M1 would not even scratch a fort like this.

C. A GI provides cover with his M1 as a medic crawls forward to tend to wounded men at Madiers, France on September 5, 1944.

With an 8-round clip attached to his cotton-web sling and a discarded pack of Lucky Strike cigarettes on the edge of his foxhole, this GI takes aim with his M1 near Aachen, Germany during October 1944.

Using a natural berm for cover, these GIs of the 100th Infantry Division fire on German troops near Rosteig, France in early December 1944.

A. By late in 1943 the M1 became the standard battle rifle of the USMC. These Marines pose with their M1s during training in late 1944.

B. Window shopping in Iceland with the M1 rifle during February 1942.

C. The M1 rifle during Airborne Infantry training at Fort Benning during April 1942.

D. An American rifleman armed with the M1 Garand looks over a fallen German at Loriol, France in the summer of 1944.

Recruits strike an aggressive pose with their M1 rifles during training in 1943.

A. A GI of the 70th Infantry Division keeps his M1 rifle handy along with a pin-up girl from *Yank* Magazine in his trench position in France during February 1945.
B. A GI of the 2nd Infantry Division takes a smoke break with his M1 close at hand among the hedgerows of Normandy during the summer of 1944.
C. A 5th Army infantryman fighting among the ruins of Cisterna, Italy during May 1944.
D. Clean weapons shoot straight: a GI of the 4th Infantry Division cleans his M1 rifle outside Duren, Germany during February 1945.

A. Just before the storm: A GI of the 7th Infantry Division on field exercises with an M1 rifle during November 1941.
B. A GI with an M1 on guard duty at a US Army installation inside Germany in the late winter of 1945. Note his cold weather gear and the M1 bayonet.

A. Men of the 7th Infantry Division talk with natives on Carlson Island during January 1944.

B. A Marine armed with an M1 rifle keeps watch for Japanese infiltrators on Cape Gloucester, January 1944. Note he carries his extra ammunition in a bandolier across his chest.

C. Hanging out the washing on the Siegfried Line: GIs enjoy a little "plunder" from a captured German bunker in France during September 1944.

A. A USMC scout-sniper team training with the M1 and M1903 Springfield rifles during August 1942. Note that they wear an early version of the "frogskin" camouflage suit.
B. Targeting Japanese snipers on Guam during August 1944, this Marine rifleman puts the accuracy of his M1 rifle to good use.
C. A portrait of a thoughtful GI of the 35th Infantry Division in Belgium during the winter of 1945. Note the camouflage net on his helmet and that he still wears a light field jacket despite the winter cold.

All the comforts of home: this GI of the 79th Infantry Division enjoys a warm stove in his bunker, a "liberated" beer stein, and a rifle rest for his M1. Germany, January 1945.

A. Better than walking: these GIs of the 63rd Infantry Division have "liberated" a surrey in Bubingen, Germany during March 1945.
B. A portrait of an American infantryman near the end of the war in Europe – a GI of the 69th Infantry Division in Germany, March 1945.

A. An officer armed with an M1 rifle supervises a little sign painting with the 83rd Infantry Division at Walternienburg, Germany April 23, 1945.

B. Mail Call: Men of the 84th Infantry Division enjoy letters from home inside a Belgian cow barn during January 1945.

C. Meaningless graffiti: A GI of the 90th Infantry Division enjoys a meal despite the Nazi slogans painted on the wall behind him at Binsfeld, Luxembourg January 31, 1945.

A Marine poses with his M1 rifle aboard the wreck of a Japanese A6M5 Model 52 "Zeke" on Cape Gloucester in January 1944.

Troops of a rifle company with M1 rifles dug in on New Guinea during 1943. Note the ammunition bandoliers and the fragmentation grenades at the ready on the log parapet.

M1941 Johnson Rifle & M1941 Johnson Light Machine Gun

Today, the Johnson rifle is among the least known of all World War II firearms. Yet on December 18, 1940, *Life* Magazine described the Johnson rifle in an article about National Defense with a headline reading "Johnson rifle stirs up great military squabble." All of this stemmed from the great debate going on within military circles about the merits of the Johnson rifle versus the M1 Garand rifle.

The Johnson rifle was designed and developed by Melvin Johnson, a junior Marine Corps Reserve officer. In May 1940 the Johnson-Garand controversy reached its zenith with a shoot-off to demonstrate the effectiveness of both weapons to a gathering of senators and high-ranking military officials. While the competition showed the great capabilities of both rifles, it closed the door on any Army acceptance of the Johnson rifle. However, the Marine Corps was late to adopt the M1 Garand and the USMC looked to the Johnson rifle as a supplemental weapon.

The Johnson rifle was chambered for the standard .30-06 cartridge, and featured a 10-round rotary magazine that created a slight bulge on the belly of the rifle. The unique rotary magazine could be reloaded with the bolt closed – a "topping off" feature that the M1 Garand lacked. The Johnson rifle's barrel could also be easily removed and this made it attractive to the newly formed USMC paratroop units. Melvin Johnson originally sold approximately 70,000 of the rifles to the Dutch government, but very few were delivered before the Japanese overran the Dutch East Indies. The remaining Dutch order rifles were taken over by the Marines.

The Johnson rifle saw very little combat service with the USMC, mostly deploying to the Solomon Islands with the First Parachute Battalion and the Marine Raiders in the region. Although an interesting design, the Johnson rifle proved rather fragile for combat, and it was soon withdrawn from frontline service. Photos of the rifle in service are very rare, and we are happy to present the first clear image of the Johnson rifle in a combat zone.

Melvin Johnson also developed a .30 caliber light machine gun, and as it was a magazine-fed weapon that could be fired from the shoulder, it was classified as an "automatic rifle" like the BAR. It was a futuristic looking weapon for the time with a high front sight, ventilated barrel shroud and a pistol grip. It was light, weighing less than 12.5 pounds without a loaded magazine (which was considerably less than a BAR). Capacity of the side-mounted magazine was 20 rounds. The Johnson Light Machine Gun M1941 was issued to Marine Corps units (including Paramarines and Raiders) and the guns were well thought of in USMC service. The US Army also used the Johnson LMG in the joint US-Canadian First Special Service Force (1SSF) and the OSS. Reports show that the 1SSF thought highly of their "Johnny Guns" and Johnson LMG saw service on the Italian front.

Left: A Marine poses in the field with a M1941 Johnson Light Machine Gun.

An interesting comparison of Marine .30 caliber weapons, from top to bottom: the M1918A2 BAR, the M1941 Johnson LMG, the M1903 Springfield rifle and the M1 Garand rifle.

A. The 1SSF earned its fierce reputation in the mountains of Italy. This Johnson LMG gunner is seen with his cold weather gear near Radicosa, Italy in January 1944.

B. The Johnson M1941 LMG seen in training with a Paramarine at the New River, North Carolina during 1942. Note the heavy elbow pads on the Marine's special jump suit.

C. The Johnson LMG during a USMC training exercise in bunker clearing during April 1942.

A. Paramarines training at New River in April 1942. The man at the top of the wall has the M1941 Johnson LMG, while the man at the bottom has the Reising Model 55 SMG. Both were intended for use with USMC paratroops.

B. Interesting view of the M1941 Johnson LMG in training with the Marine Corps. The Johnson LMG was much lighter and handier than the BAR, but offered no greater fire power or accuracy.

A. The Johnson M1941 LMG on the obstacle course at USMC New River.
B. Rare view of a Marine Corps "photo shoot" featuring a USMC paratrooper armed with the M1941 Johnson LMG. Note the Marine's odd parachute "jump helmet".
C. A second view from the same field demonstration. The man at the left holds a Reising Model 55 folding stock SMG.

A. The M1941 Johnson LMG posed with a Paramarine in frog skin camouflage during 1943.
B. An exceptionally rare view of the Johnson M1941 rifle (left), in use with the Marine Parachute Regiment in the Solomon Islands. The Marine on the right holds the Johnson M1941 LMG. *(Author's collection)*

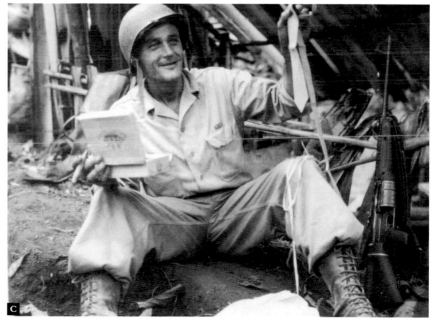

A. A Marine Corps photo of the M1941 Johnson rifle after its acceptance into USMC service in March 1942. Note the use of 5-round chargers to load the .30 caliber ammunition into the rifle's 10-round rotary magazine. **B.** A gas-mask protected Marine training with the Johnson LMG at USMC New River during 1942.
C. Major Harry Torgerson of the 1st Marine Parachute Regiment displays the new tie he received for Christmas while on Bougainville, December 1943. In the background is his M1941 Johnson LMG. Major Torgerson was a major proponent of the weapon.

Shotguns

The combat shotgun is a wholly American invention. American troops wielded shotguns during World War I, prompting the Kaiser's government to lodge a formal complaint, claiming their use in combat was "illegal" and caused undue pain and suffering. This ridiculous accusation was quickly overcome and the 12 gauge Trench Gun, Model of 1917 became an important, if somewhat unknown part of the American arsenal. Equipped with a "ventilated rib" hand guard above the barrel, as well as a bayonet lug, the Trench Gun is a fearsome looking weapon.

As World War II came about, the need for shotguns in the US military grew. Predominant use of combat shotguns came in the Pacific Theater, where the jungle terrain dictated much close quarter fighting. The Marine Corps was the primary user and employed shotguns in almost every Pacific Theater campaign. Shotgun use in the European and Mediterranean theatres was quite limited, but in specialized roles there was no substitute for the "scattergun" which was found to be particularly intimidating to prisoners. In the Pacific, shotguns found their niche in patrol duty, often blasting away foliage to reveal enemy positions and were also particularly helpful in breaking up Japanese "Banzai" charges.

Shotgun drawbacks were two-fold: the obvious limitations in their range and the susceptibility of the shotgun ammunition to damage from moisture. Almost all of the 00 Buckshot shells were made of heavy paper, and if they got wet they would swell and no longer fit into the chamber. Brass-cased shotgun shells were designed but most of the brass shotgun ammunition did not reach the troops until very late in the war.

Many shotguns were used in supporting roles, including guarding prisoners, bases and supplies. Stateside use of shotguns allowed valuable rifles and submachine guns to be deployed overseas. American combat shotguns made a quiet but important contribution to the war effort, filling a niche role like no other firearm could.

Left: USMC combat photographers, the Jones twins (Eugene and Charles) seen on Iwo Jima. On the left is the Winchester Model 97 Trench Gun, and on the right the M1 Carbine.

Two Marines armed with Winchester Model 97 Trench Guns moving past a blasted Japanese bunker on Roi–Namur Island during early February 1944.

A. A Marine with a Winchester Model 97 Trench Gun covers a M1 flamethrower team on Saipan, July 12, 1944.

B. Army troops with the Winchester Model 97 Trench Gun along with a Thompson M1928 submachine gun. Note the early-war style pith helmets.

C. GIs on Bougainville armed with the Model 97 Trench Gun and the M1 Carbine.

D. A Marine carries a Winchester Model 97 Trench Gun ashore on Okinawa.

Shotguns are rarely photographed in the combat zones in Europe. In this photo two Army nurses are quite well protected by Army MPs in Normandy. At the far left an MP carries the rare Stevens M520-30 Trench Gun.

Two views of a stateside guard armed with the Remington Model 31 Riot Gun. The use of shotguns for guard duty in the States allowed valuable rifles and machine guns to be sent to combat units. *(Author's collection)*

Two views of a Marine guard armed with a Winchester Model 97 Trench Gun keeping watch on the 4th Marine Division brig during January 1944.

A. A skeet shooting competition aboard the carrier *Yorktown* between a Remington Model 11 semi-automatic (training gun) shotgun and the Winchester Model 97 Trench Gun.

B. A Marine armed with a Winchester Model 97 Trench Gun follows a Thompson gunner into action on Saipan during June 1944.

C. A Marine attaches a M1917 bayonet to his Model 97 Trench Gun. Camp Pendleton, California in December 1943. The Model 97 equipped with a bayonet is a fearsome-looking weapon.

A. Marine war dog handlers on Iwo Jima armed with the Model 97 Trench Gun and the M1 Carbine.

B. Marine combat photographers take a break on Saipan with a Winchester Model 97 Trench Gun close at hand.

C. A Marine war dog handler armed with a Remington Model 12 Trench Gun outside a Japanese bunker on Iwo Jima.

A Marine armed with a Winchester Model 12 Trench Gun going over the seawall on Okinawa, April 1, 1945. The pouches on his uniform are a grenade vest, sometimes used by Marines to carry shotgun ammunition.

Browning Automatic Rifle

Designed by the legendary John M. Browning, the Browning Automatic Rifle (BAR) debuted in American service during late 1918 in the trenches of the Western Front in France. After making quite an impression in World War, I the M1918 BAR began a slow transformation from a shoulder-fired automatic rifle to a cobbled-up light machine gun. The M1918A2 BAR featured a bipod and flash hider, a hinged butt plate, a carrying handle and a single stabilizing pod for the butt stock. All of these fashionable accoutrements for a 1930s era light machine gun added up to little more than a lot of extra weight for very little gain in performance. With everything added, the BAR's weight grew to more than 20 pounds. The BAR is a fine automatic rifle, but it is most certainly not a light machine gun. Marine and Army BAR men quickly discarded or conveniently "lost" the added weight (the bipod alone weighed almost 2.5 pounds).

The BAR fires the standard American World War II service round—the .30-06 cartridge. While somewhat limited in sustained automatic fire by its 20-round magazine capacity, the accuracy and penetrating power of its .30 caliber ammunition made it a highly respected weapon on the battlefield. Coupled with the semi-automatic M1 rifle the BAR provided the "base of fire", giving American infantry more firepower than any other combatant nation.

Marine units added more and more BARs as the war progressed, and also modified them on occasion to include a vertical fore-grip to protect the gunner's fingers from the red-hot barrel. Although the weapon lacked a quick-change barrel and thus was limited in its sustained fire capacity, the BAR was used to great effect throughout World War II. The BAR is a very robust weapon and is exceptionally reliable. GIs may have cursed it for its weight, but when the firefights were over they easily forgave the gun's small collection of faults

The BAR remained in service until the early 1960s and even served in some capacity in the Vietnam War. This is a classic American firearm, a remarkable design that served for almost five decades and represents one of the finest automatic weapon designs of all time.

Left: A Marine BAR gunner in action on Okinawa during May 1945. Note the large amount of magazine pouches he carries, evidence that his weapon is almost constantly in use.

A. A Marine using the BAR on the shell-blasted landscape of Wana Ridge on Okinawa.
B. GIs of the 82nd Airborne in action with the BAR in Belgium during December 1944.
C. This BAR man of the 1st Infantry Division takes a break to write a few lines to the folks back home. Belgium, January 1945.

A. A BAR man defending a USMC position on Okinawa during May 1945.

B. A BAR gunner of the 13th Infantry Regiment of the 8th Infantry Division in action at La Haye Du Puits, France in July 1944. Note that he carries his extra BAR magazines in a bandolier.

C. A BAR gunner of the 76th Infantry Division at Echternach, Belgium in December 1944.

A. This stone-faced BAR man of the 2nd Infantry Division is reported to have killed 27 Germans with his weapon in France during the summer of 1944.

B. This PFC of the 3rd Infantry Division used his BAR to drive off an entire column of German troops at Rochefort, Belgium in January 1945.

A USMC BAR gunner stalking Japanese snipers on Bougainville. The power of the BAR's .30 caliber ammunition proved to be quite an advantage in jungle fighting.

A. Posed for the camera, these Marines show how they flushed Japanese troops out of the many caves of Okinawa. The BAR gunners provided useful covering fire during these deadly attacks.
B. The paratrooper has fired his BAR enough to cause the wooden fore-end to start to smoke. Corregidor, February 1945.
C. A Marine armed with a BAR on patrol in thick jungle of Bougainville, December 1943.

The American infantry squad possessed more firepower than any other army's infantry section in World War II. The base of that firepower came from the weapons seen here with the 102nd Infantry Division – the .30 caliber M1 rifle and the .30 caliber Browning Automatic Rifle. Germany, Spring 1945.

A. Ducking under Japanese fire, this Marine BAR gunner moves into position outside of Garapan, Saipan during June 1944.

B. This Marine BAR man on Guam in August 1944 has reduced the weight of his weapon by removing the bipod, flash hider and carrying handle from his gun. This was a common practice for BAR men no matter where they served.

C. Engaging German snipers at range in Harze, Belgium January 1945.

This BAR gunner of the American Division killed ten Japanese troops near Hill 260 on Bougainville.

A USMC BAR man on the barren island of Peleliu. The Marines normally used the BAR as an automatic rifle, the role it was designed for, as opposed to a light machine gun.

As the war progressed, many Marine units modified their BARs to include a pistol grip on the fore-end of the stock. This was to give the gunner a better forward grip and help prevent him from burning his fingers when the barrel became hot enough to smolder the wooden fore-end.

A Marine BAR gunner engages Japanese troops dug in on Wana Ridge, Okinawa. The man at left is preparing to throw a hand grenade.

A. The BAR on guard duty among the rooftops of Tunis during 1943.

B. A Marine BAR man on Guadalcanal awaits another Japanese attack in late 1942.

C. A Bazooka team of the 90th Infantry Division credited with knocking out a German "Panther" tank at Metz in October 1944. The BAR man kept the German infantry pinned while the Bazooka team did its work.

The BAR struggled in some respects when forced to fit into the light machine gun role. Sustained fire was a challenge, with no provision for quick barrel changes and only a 20-round magazine. Much of the time BAR men removed the bipod and flash hider to save weight.

A Marine BAR gunner takes a quick nap during the fighting on Okinawa. The fore-end on his BAR has been reworked in a USMC ordnance shop to include a pistol grip.

A Marine BAR gunner on Okinawa. His weapon is fitted with a leather sling and he carries a pair of Mark II fragmentation grenades.

A recruit learns to use the M1918A2 Browning Automatic Rifle. Heavy, but remarkably accurate and reliable, the BAR earned great respect from allies and enemies alike.

Browning .30 Caliber Machine Guns

The Water-Cooled M1917A1: Designed by America's arms genius, John M. Browning, the .30 caliber M1917 was a heavy, tripod-mounted, water-cooled machine gun in league with the Maxim, Schwarzlose, MG08 and Vickers guns of the early 20th Century. About 30,000 M1917 MGs were sent to France for service with the AEF during 1918. In less than a year of combat in World War I, the Browning M1917 established itself as the finest heavy machine gun in the world.

A number of small modifications were made during the late 1930s to produce the M1917A1. While incredibly stable and accurate, the M1917A1 was very heavy: the gun weighed 41 pounds with water in the cooling jacket and the tripod added another 52 pounds. Ammunition was fed in via 250-round cloth belts from wooden ammunition boxes. As long as water was kept in the cooling jacket and ammunition was available, the M1917A1 could be expected to keep right on shooting. Marines used the continuous firepower provided by the M1917 guns to break up Japanese "Banzai" charges and Army units often used the long-range accuracy of the guns to support infantry advances in Europe.

The M1917A1 was standard equipment for both Army and Marine heavy weapons companies and the weapon served throughout the war with distinction. The water-cooled guns can also be seen mounted on Jeeps and other light vehicles to provide greater mobility. The M1917A1 continued to provide sterling service through the Korean War. It is likely the finest sustained-fire weapon ever produced.

The Air-Cooled M1919A4: The Browning air-cooled .30 caliber machine guns were developed from the lessons learned during World War I. Using essentially the same operating system as the M1917, the M1919 guns featured a ventilated cooling jacket around the barrel. This created a much lighter gun (31 pounds) that used a lighter tripod (the M2 tripod weighed 14 pounds). The air-cooled guns were much easier to carry and could be deployed forward during an infantry attack. Once America went on the offensive during World War II, the Browning air-cooled guns were usually the first machine guns available on a beachhead or during an advance.

The M1919A4 was adopted in the 1930s and almost 400,000 guns were produced by the end of World War II. Like the M1917, it was a belt-fed gun using 250-round cloth and later disintegrating metal link belts. While not a true "heavy machine gun" the M1919A4 was not a light machine gun either. An attempt to turn the M1919A4 into a light machine gun brought about the M1919A6 which featured a detachable butt stock, a folding bipod, a carrying handle and a lighter barrel. These modifications shaved off almost 12 ½ pounds from the weight of a M1919A4. The M1919A6 was a compromise at best, which partially fulfilled an immediate need but was never fully satisfactory.

The Browning M1919A4 is one of the classic infantry weapons of World War II, earning great praise from the troops who used it in action, and the M1919A4 remained in service throughout the Korean War and into the Vietnam War era.

Left: The Browning .30 caliber M1917A1 machine gun with the 102nd Infantry Division at Uerdingen, Germany during March, 1945. This gun is equipped with a simple flash hider on the muzzle.

A. An M1917 machine gun position set up in the Ardennes forest in January 1945. Note the grenades at the ready in the foreground.

B. GIs with an M1917 machine gun on the French-German border in early 1945.

C. A Marine sets up the water-cooled M1917A1 MG on a later model M2 tripod. Note the "Kabar" fighting knife on his belt. Iwo Jima, March 1945.

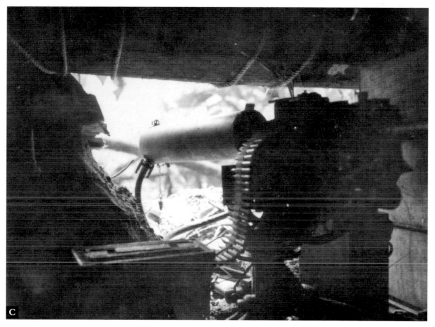

A. Machine gunners of the 36th Infantry Division with rudimentary camouflage for themselves and their M1917A1 machine gun. Bischwiller, France in January 1945.
B. The M1917 machine gun was capable of incredible feats of sustained fire and was one of the best defensive weapons of the war. This Marine machine gun has been firing extensively on Okinawa.
C. The M1917A1 shown in the tight confines of an MG bunker on Bougainville, November 1943.

Men of the 30th Infantry Division digging in with their M1917A1 on Sicily.

A. Lifting the heavy M1917A1 MG on to the M1917 tripod near Mount Grande, Italy during February 1945.
B. A gruff-looking Marine shoulders a M1917A1 along a muddy jungle trail on Cape Gloucester in January 1944.
C. A Marine carrying the 50-plus pound M1917 tripod for the M1917A1 MG uphill on Guam, summer 1944. Note he also carries an M1 Carbine.

Men of the 13th Armored Division set up a M1917A1 machine gun near Braunau, Germany in late April 1945.

A. An M1917A1 equipped with a flash hider in position with the 100th Infantry Division outside Aachen, Germany during December 1944.
B. A M1917A1 MG of the 8th Infantry Division set up to cover the street below in Schweilm, Germany during April 1945.
C. GIs examine a captured Japanese Type 11 light machine gun in their M1917A1 gun bunker along the Burma Road in February 1945.
D. Marines firing an M1917A1 MG outside of Naha, Okinawa. Note the steam condensing hose attached to the canteen.

GIs of the 133rd Engineering Battalion with a M1917A1 MG set up to defend a bridge in Northern France during October 1944.

Men of the "Galahad Forces" with their Browning M1917A1 operating in Burma during 1944. Note the perforations in the simple M3 "beer can" flash-hider attached to the muzzle.

A. Prepared for invasion: an M1917 on an AA tripod set up at La Guardia airport in New York City during early 1942. *(Author's collection)*

B. The M1917A1 MG mounted on a pedestal in an Army Jeep.

C. The M1917A1 machine gun carried on a pedestal mount in a light truck. Newfoundland, May 1942.

A M1919A4 MG position at Anzio, February 1944. Note the MKII fragmentation grenade and the binoculars on the sandbags.

A. A .30 caliber Browning M1919A4 on the M2 tripod mount with the Marines on Guam during July 1944.

B. A M1919A6 (with shoulder stock removed) mounted on an M2 tripod with the 442nd Infantry Regiment in the Vosges region of France, October 1944.

C. Marines on Iwo Jima with a M1919A4, equipped with a field-manufactured carrying handle.

A. An M1919A4 and M1 rifles cover a large prisoner of war camp in Germany during April 1945.

B. A Marine MG crew with their M1919A4 in the Southwest Pacific. The gunner's shoulder pad was used to provide protection from the hot barrel when carried on the shoulder.

C. The M2 tripod allowed the Browning M1919A4 to be set up very low to the ground. Seen here in use by Marine Raiders on New Guinea.

D. Marines firing at Japanese positions on Okinawa. Note the gunner's .45 caliber M1911A1 pistol and machete.

A. A photo for the folks back home: a young recruit poses with the Browning M1919A4 gun on the M2 tripod. *(Author's collection)*

B. An M1919A6, mounted on an M2 tripod with 2nd Infantry Division in Belgium during January 1945.

C. GIs of the 30th Infantry Division using an M1919A6 MG at Kohlscheid, Germany on October 16, 1944. The M1919A6 concept was compromise between a light and medium machine gun.

A. A machine gunner the 77th Infantry Division carries the M1919A6 on Okinawa. Note that the gun has the pintle attached (which mounts the gun to the M2 tripod).

B. A communications man uses a BD–71 six–line telephone switchboard with a Browning M1919A4 MG resting nearby in Northern France, Fall 1944.

A. A Marine MG team posed with their Browning M1919A4 .30 caliber gun on an M2 tripod.
B. The M1919A4 on a M2 tripod with the 10th Armored Division near Ulm, Germany in April 1945.
C. The Browning M1919A6 mounted on the M2 tripod in Germany during the spring of 1945.

A. A happy GI of the 35th Infantry Division dug in with his M1919A4 MG at Geilenkirchen, Germany during February 1945.
B. US infantry training for the invasion of Europe with the M1919A4 at the Beach Assault Training Center in England, December 1943.

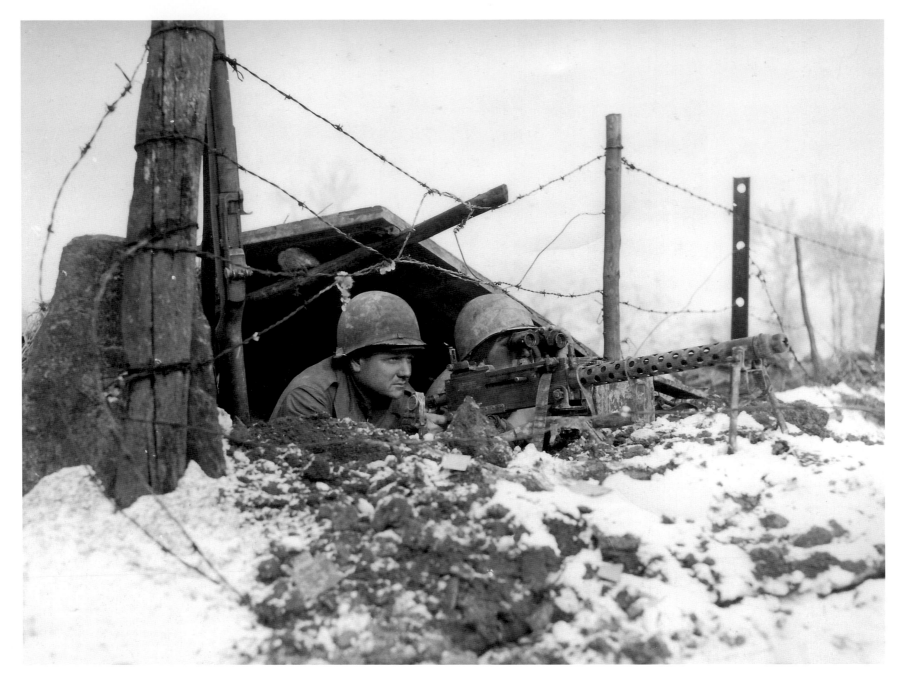

A Browning M1919A6 mounted on the M2 tripod with the 82nd Airborne, near Odrimont, Belgium January 1945.

A. GIs of the 30th Infantry Division use their M1919A4 in the tough street fighting in Aachen, Germany during October 1944. This was the first major German city to fall to Allied forces.

B. Men of the 7th Infantry Division help secure the beachhead at Kwajalein Atoll with their Browning M1919A4.

C. A Browning M1919A4 of the 1st Marine Division on Okinawa, May 2, 1945. Note the low profile of the M2 tripod.

A Browning M1919A4 of an Army Air Corps unit provides perimeter security on Randolph Field in the Philippines during early 1945.

The Browning machine guns proved reliable regardless of the weather conditions. This frozen M1919A4 is seen with the 5th Armored Division in the Ardennes during December, 1944.

Troops defending the California coast in early 1942 with the M1919A4 set up for anti-aircraft use on the M1917A1 tripod.

A. The Browning M1919A4 mounted on 24th Infantry Division Jeep on Mindanao Island during April 1945. Any of the Browning machine guns could be found mounted on almost any type of US vehicle.
B. This M1919A4 is mounted just ahead of the commander's hatch on a Sherman tank. Note the tanker's non-standard coffee pot atop the GI cooking stove.
C. The M1919A4 MGs were frequently mounted on the M3 Halftrack as seen here in Germany during the spring of 1945.

Browning .50 Caliber Machine Guns

The Browning .50 caliber machine gun was a product of advanced weapons technology, coupled with American experience in World War I. During the Great War the German Army was the first to develop anti-tank weapons (as they were the first to face tanks in combat). One of their developments to counter the early Allied tanks was a massive 13.2mm bolt-action rifle. Captured examples of the German "T-Gewehr" were brought home and analyzed, and soon the new .50 caliber (12.7mm) round was born. Using scaled up technology from his .30 caliber M1917 and M1919 machine gun designs, Browning created the water-cooled M1921 .50 caliber machine gun. During the 1920s and early 1930s modifications were made to create the air-cooled M2HB (heavy barrel) machine gun. The .50 caliber M2 HB is still in service today, with only minor modifications made since World War II – a remarkable lifespan for an infantry weapon.

The .50 caliber M2 is truly a heavy machine gun. The gun (with a 45-inch barrel) weighs 81 pounds and the M3 tripod adds another 44 pounds. The power and range of the weapon (striking accurately out to 2,000 yards) easily make up for any complaints about weight. In World War II the .50 caliber guns could easily destroy all but the most hardened targets, and were capable of knocking out light armored vehicles. Their performance as anti-aircraft guns was exceptional and many of the water-cooled .50 caliber M2 guns were used in this role. Ammunition for the Browning M2 included ball, incendiary, armor-piercing and tracer rounds, fed by 120-round metallic link belts.

The greatest challenge that the troops faced with .50 caliber guns was in jungle or mountain combat as the effort to move the massive guns into position was an incredible chore. As the photos in this book show, more often than not the troops found a way to get the .50 caliber MGs wherever they needed them. Whenever possible the .50 caliber MGs were mounted on Jeeps, trucks or halftracks and the added mobility further enhanced their capabilities.

No other combatant nation in World War II fielded a weapon in any numbers that could match the Browning .50 caliber guns. To this day, the Browning .50 caliber M2 machine gun can dominate a battlefield, and is likely to do so for some time to come.

Left: Marines with a Browning M2 .50 caliber machine gun mounted on an M3 tripod on the beach at Kwajalein, February 1, 1944.

A. GIs of the 35th Infantry Division with the Browning .50 caliber M2, set up as an infantry machine gun. This view shows the details of the massive M3 tripod (which weighs 44 pounds) which is still in use today.

B. GIs on the range with the Browning M2 .50 caliber MG. Note the man to the right with a BAR.

C. The .50 caliber M2 gun and the M3 tripod is truly a heavy machine gun, weighing almost 128 pounds. This MG team is seen at Fort Custer, Michigan shortly before the war.

A. Troops in training with the Browning M2 .50 caliber MG. This gun is equipped with the M1 telescopic sight.
B. A Marine .50 caliber MG position on Saipan. Note the massive belt of linked ammunition.
C. A .50 caliber MG of the 102nd Infantry Division in Germany during the spring of 1945.

A. A .50 caliber position on the French–German border during the winter of 1945. *(Author's collection)*

B. The .50 caliber MG used as artillery. Marines fire from a nearby island to support landings on Cape Torokina in late 1943.

C. The massive size and weight of the Browning M2 .50 caliber restricted its use in the infantry role. This example is in use with the 79th Infantry Division in Germany during January 1945.

A Marine machine gun bunker with the Browning .50 caliber machine gun in the Southwest Pacific.

Marines defending the Okinawa coastline with the Browning M2 .50 caliber machine gun. Note the .50 caliber ammunition in metal links in the ammunition cans.

A. Men of the 135th Field Artillery with a .50 caliber M2 gun on Bougainville during December 1943.

B. The .50 caliber MG set up as an AA gun defends Iceland in February 1942.

C. Marine Raiders using Browning M2 .50 caliber aircraft machine guns on New Georgia during 1943. The aircraft guns were lighter and faster firing than the standard infantry guns.

D. A pedestal mounted .50 caliber M2 gun on a Jeep. This vehicle has been fitted with outriggers to counteract the powerful recoil of the .50 caliber gun.

The M2 .50 caliber MG was mounted on a wide variety of US vehicles, ranging from trucks to tanks. The .50 caliber gun provided an incredible level of automatic firepower for a wide range of missions.

The M55 quadruple .50 caliber mount provided American infantry units with highly effective anti-aircraft defense against low flying enemy planes. The M2 guns were fed by 200-round "tombstone" ammunition cans.

The Browning M2 .50 caliber was also produced in a water-cooled version. This was used throughout World War II in the anti-aircraft role. Here, Marine Corps gunners relax next to their camouflage-painted Browning M2 gun on Bougainville in 1944.

A. The .50 caliber M2 in an AA position in Iceland during 1942.
B. A Marine .50 caliber AA position defending Guadalcanal in 1943.
C. The .50 caliber M2 AA gun in service with the Marine Corps in the Solomon Islands during September 1943.
D. Marines man a .50 caliber M2 AA gun on Rendova during 1943.

A. The .50 caliber M2 AA MG showing details of the M3 mount. Note the gunner's shield and the raised AA sight.

B. "Cognac", a .50 caliber M2 AA gun of the 1st Infantry Division. Belgium, January 1945.

C. The .50 caliber M2 water-cooled MG on the M3 AA mount. Note the raised AA sight. Belgium, January 1945.

Bibliography & Suggested Reading

U.S. Infantry Weapons of World War II by Bruce N. Canfield, Andrew Mobray Publishers Inc. 1994 USA

Hard Rain: History of the Browning Machine Guns by Frank Iannamico, Moose Lake Publishing 2002 USA

The Browning Machine Gun "Semper Fi Fifty" Volume IV by Frank Iannamico & Dolf L. Goldsmith, Collector Grade Publications 2008 Canada

Military Small Arms of the 20th Century by Ian V. Hogg & John Weeks, Arms & Armour Press 1977 Scotland

Small Arms of the World by Edward C. Ezell, Stackpole Books 1983 USA

Weapon Mounts For Secondary Armament Prepared for the Detroit Arsenal, Ordnance Corps, U.S. Army by G.O. Noville & Associates Inc. 1957 2nd Edition, Long Mountain Outfitters 2007 USA

The World's Submachine Guns Volume One by Thomas B. Nelson, International Small Arms Publishers 1963 Germany

United States Submachine Guns: from the American 180 to the ZX-7 by Frank Iannamico, Moose Lake Publishing 2004 USA

American Thunder: the Military Thompson Submachine Guns by Frank Iannamico, Moose Lake Publishing 2000 USA

The Gun That Made the Twenties Roar by William J. Helmer, The Gun Room Press 1969 USA

Rock in a Hard Place: The Browning Automatic Rifle by James L. Ballou, Collectors Grade Publications 2000 Canada

War Baby! The U.S. Caliber .30 Carbine by Larry L. Ruth, Collector Grade Publications 1992 Canada

International Armament Volumes I & II by George Johnson and Hans Lockhoven, International Small Arms Publishers 1965 Germany

Automatic Weapons of the World by Melvin M. Johnson Jr. & Charles T. Haven, William Morrow & Company 1945 USA

Shots Fired In Anger by Lt. Colonel John B. George, National Rifle Association of America 1981 (2nd Edition) USA

Ordnance Went Up Front by Roy F. Dunlap, Thomas G. Samworth 1948 USA

Dedicated to all the men and women
who served during the dark days
of World War II